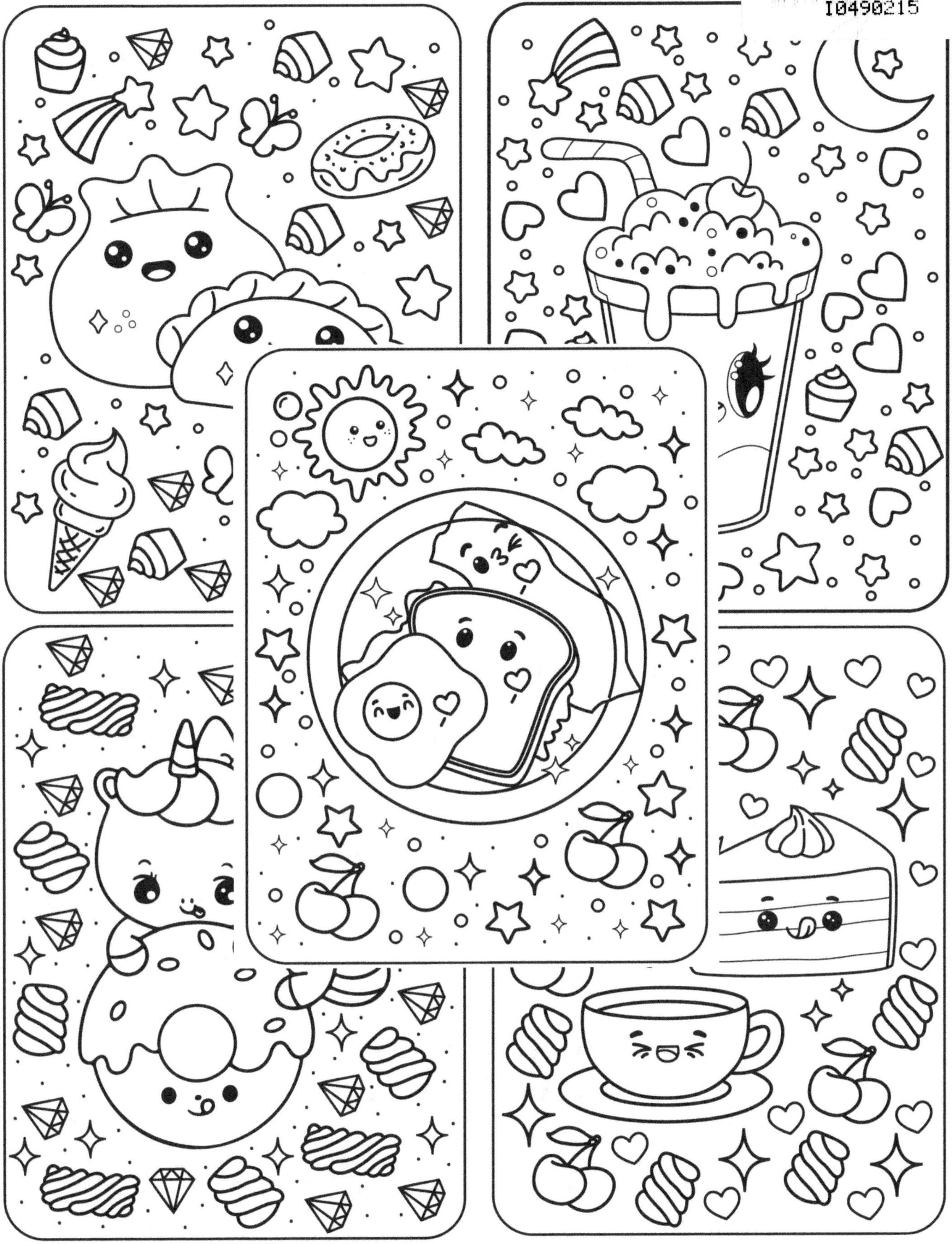

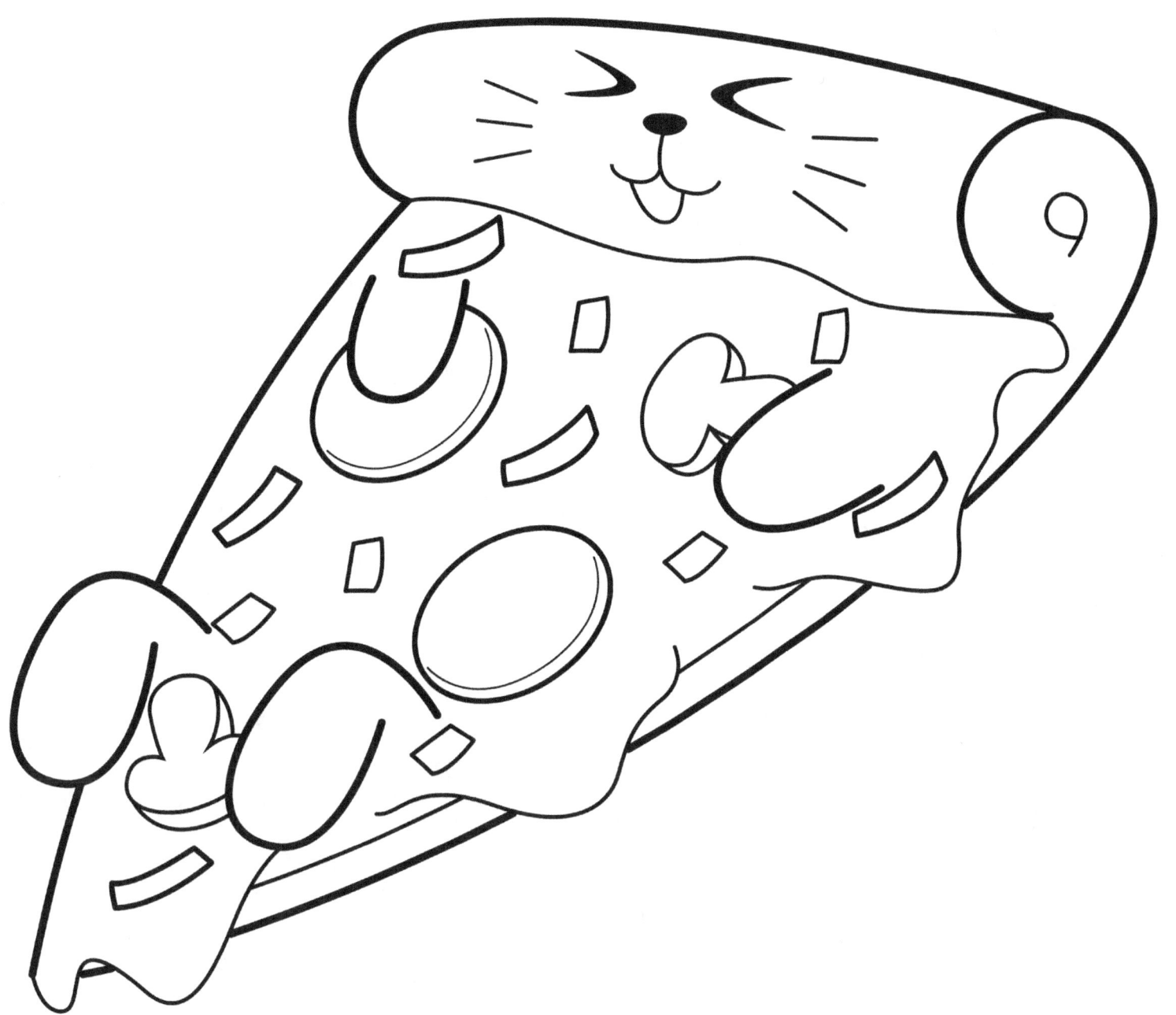

THIS BOOK BELONGS TO

_____

Adorable food
Coloring Book

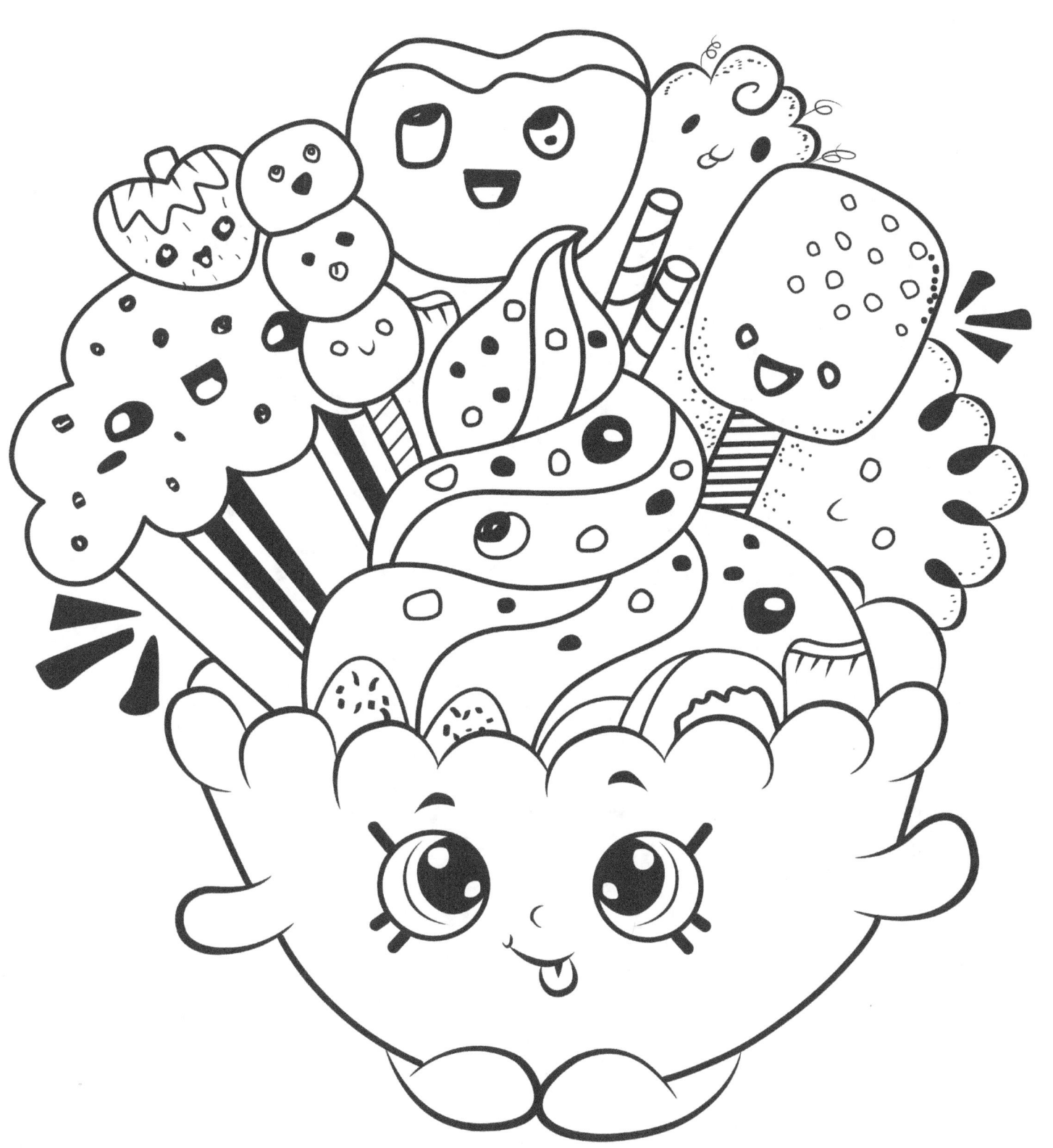

Adorable food
Coloring Book

Adorable Food
Coloring Book

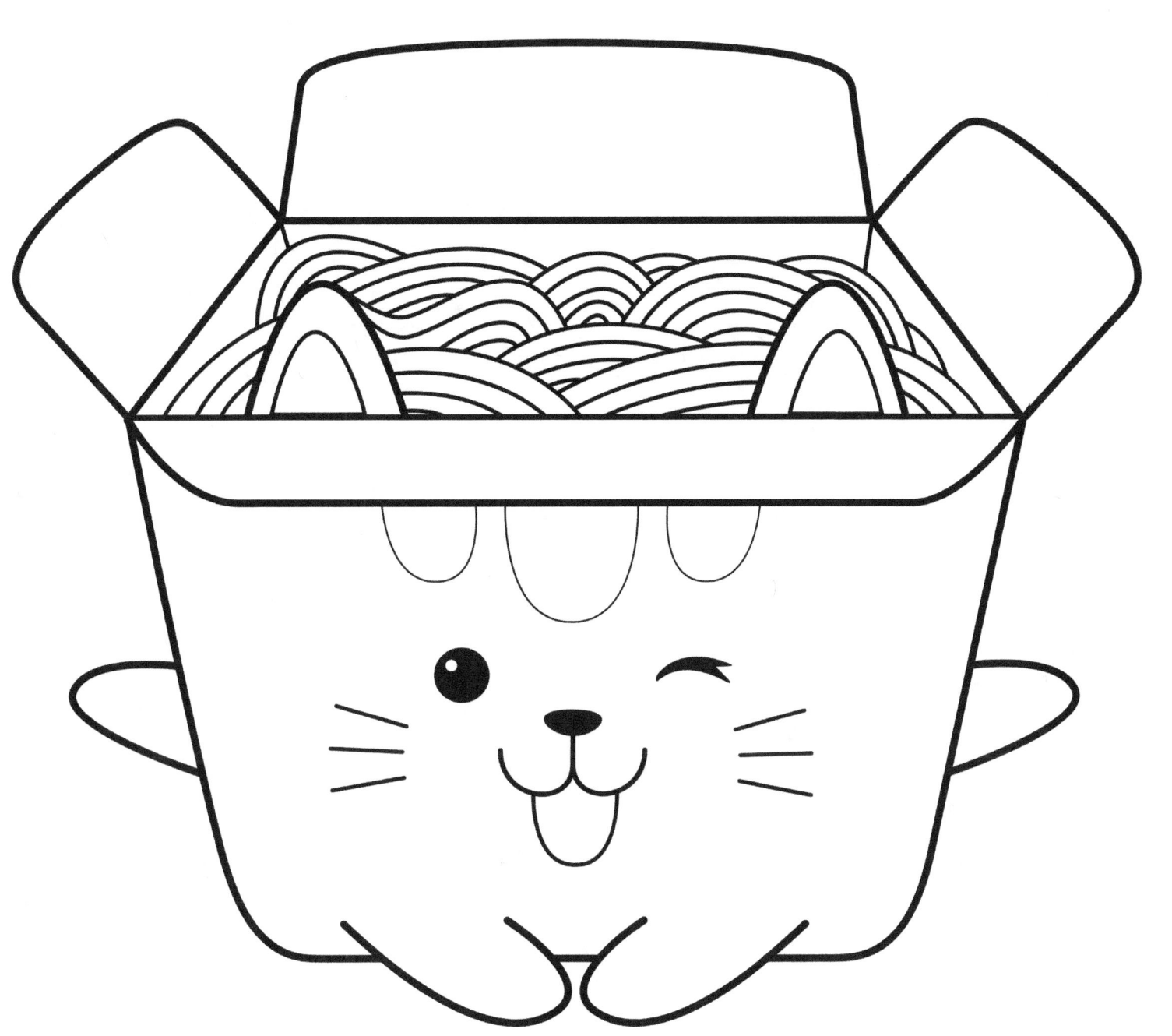

Adorable food
Coloring Book

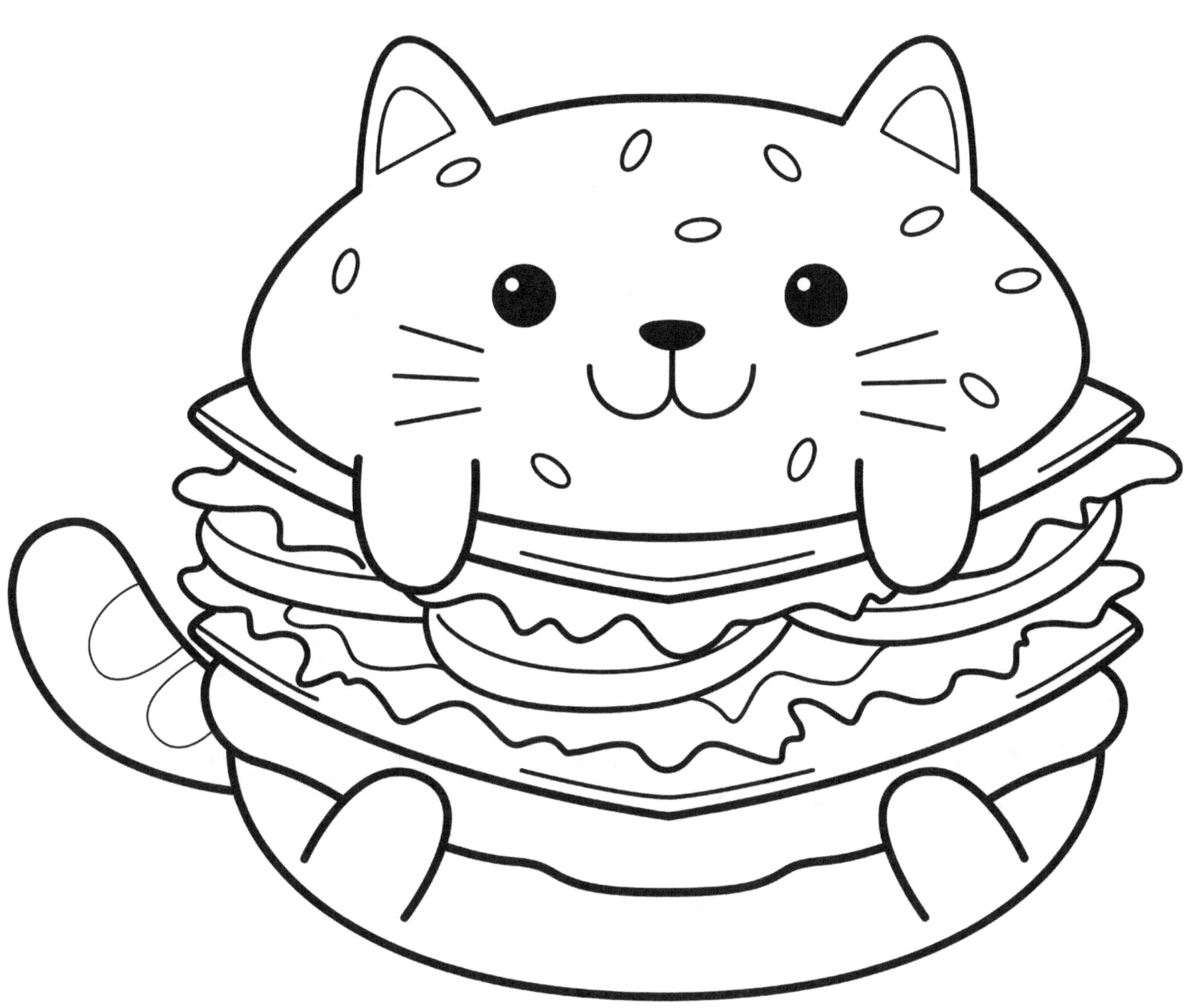

Adorable food
Coloring Book

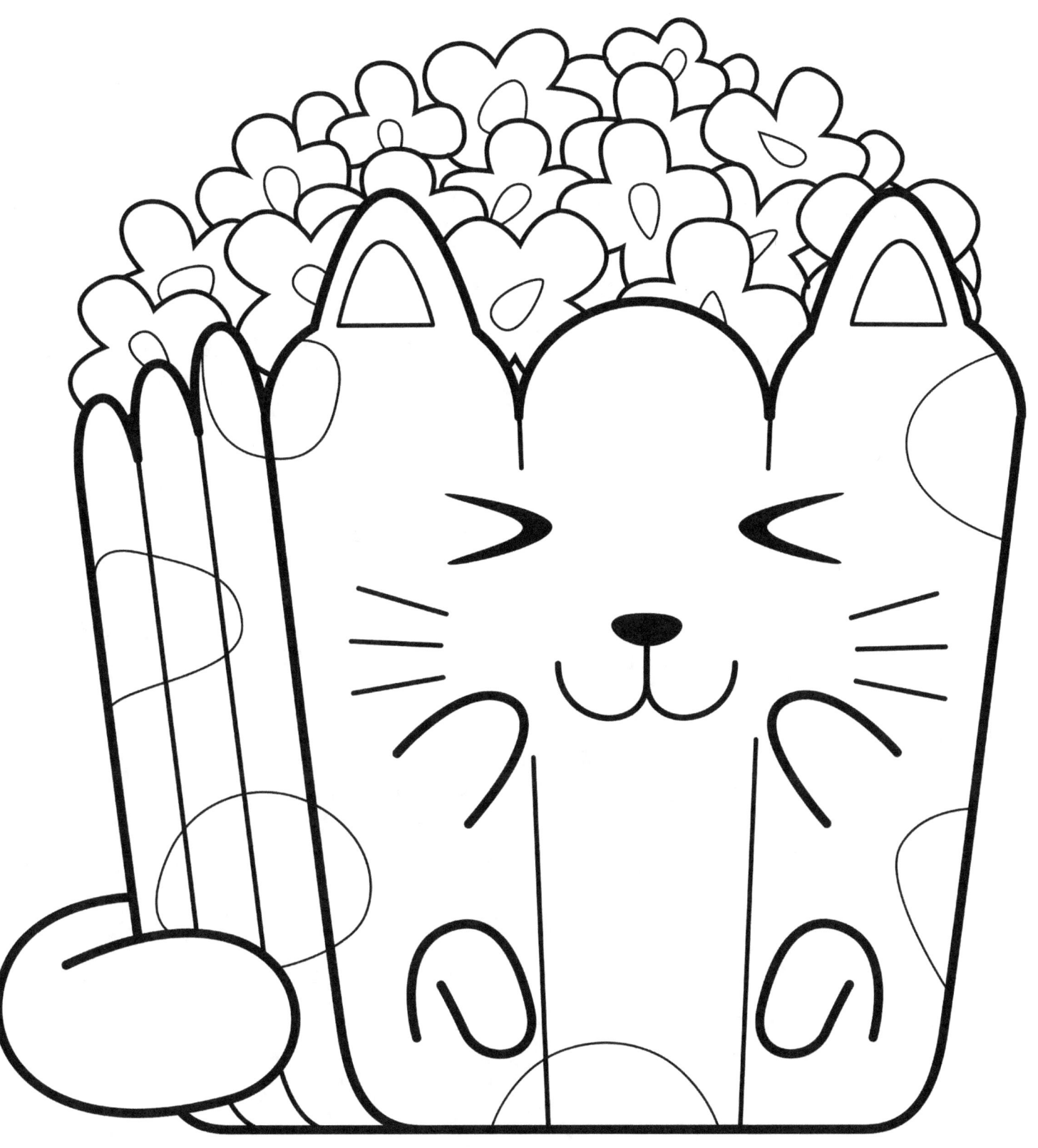

Adorable food
Coloring Book

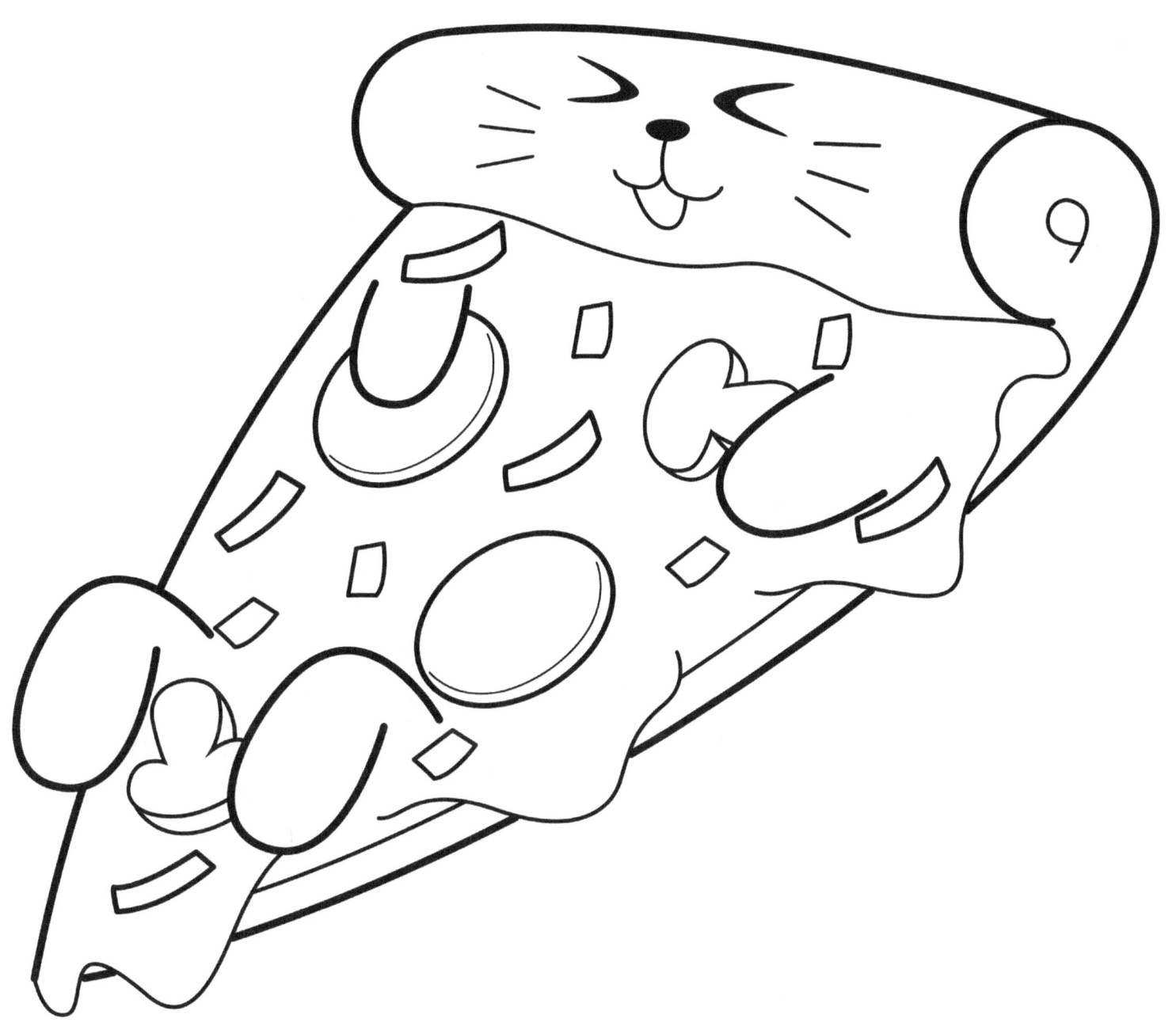

Adorable food
Coloring Book

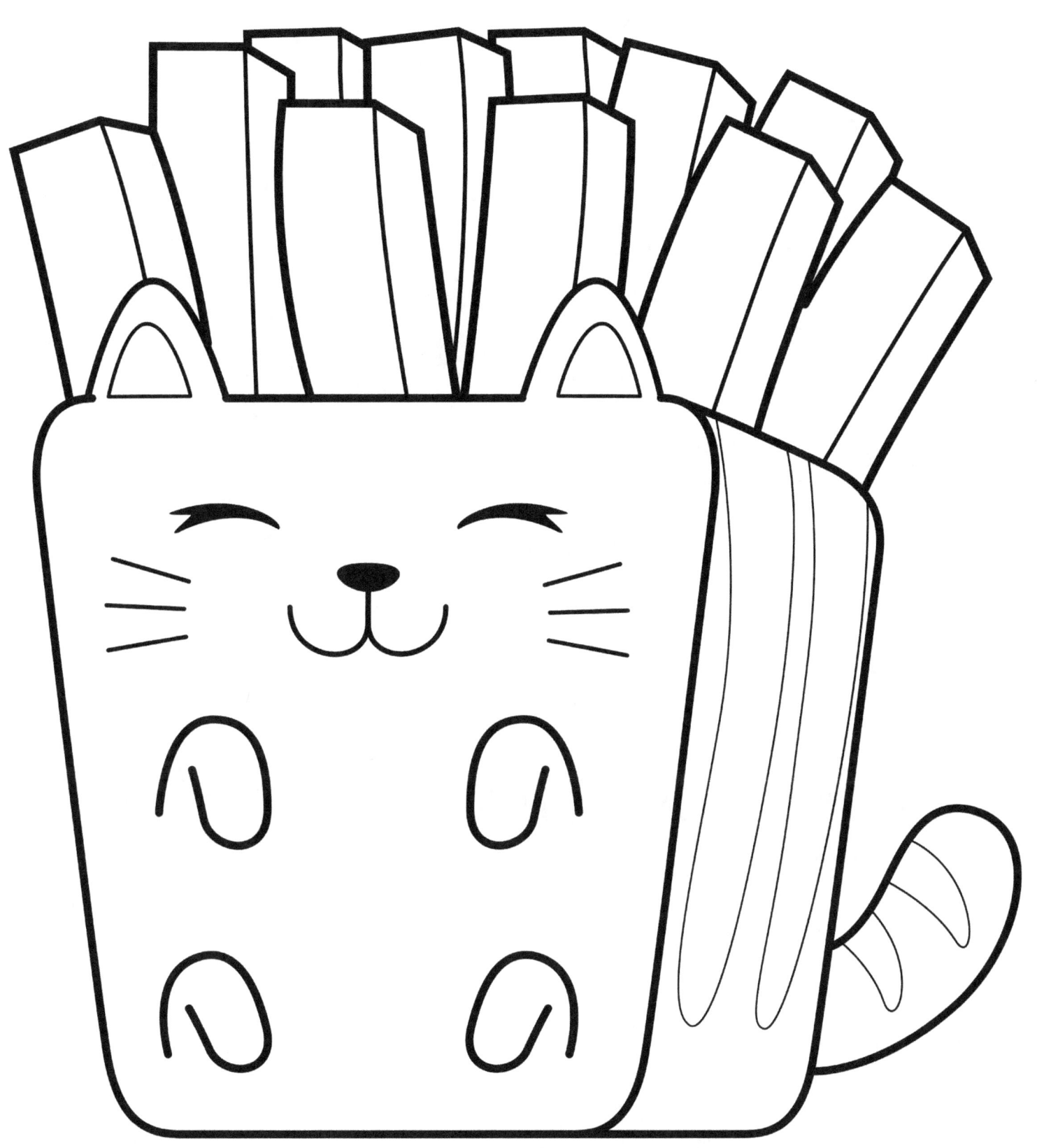

Adorable food
Coloring Book

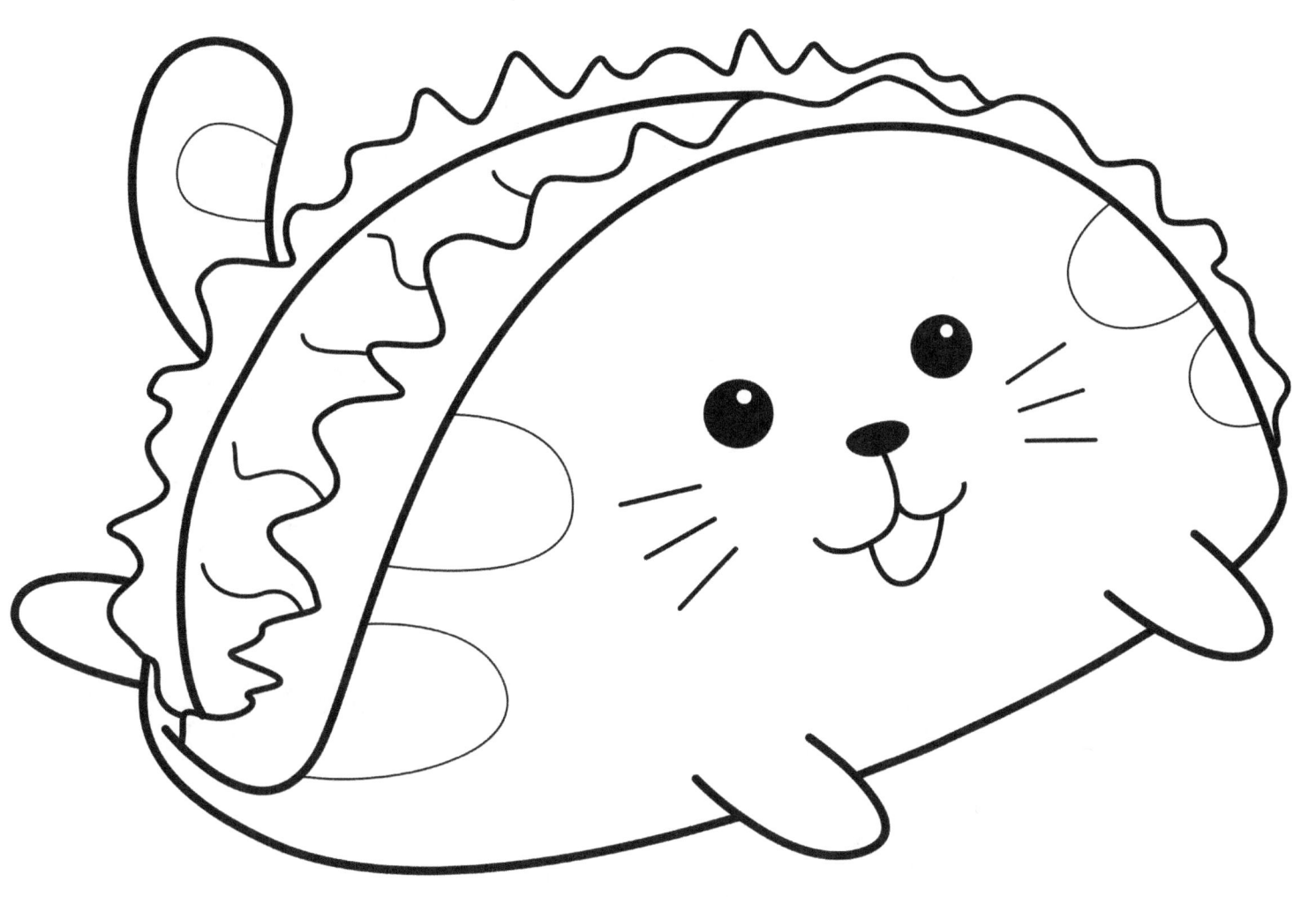

Adorable food
Coloring Book

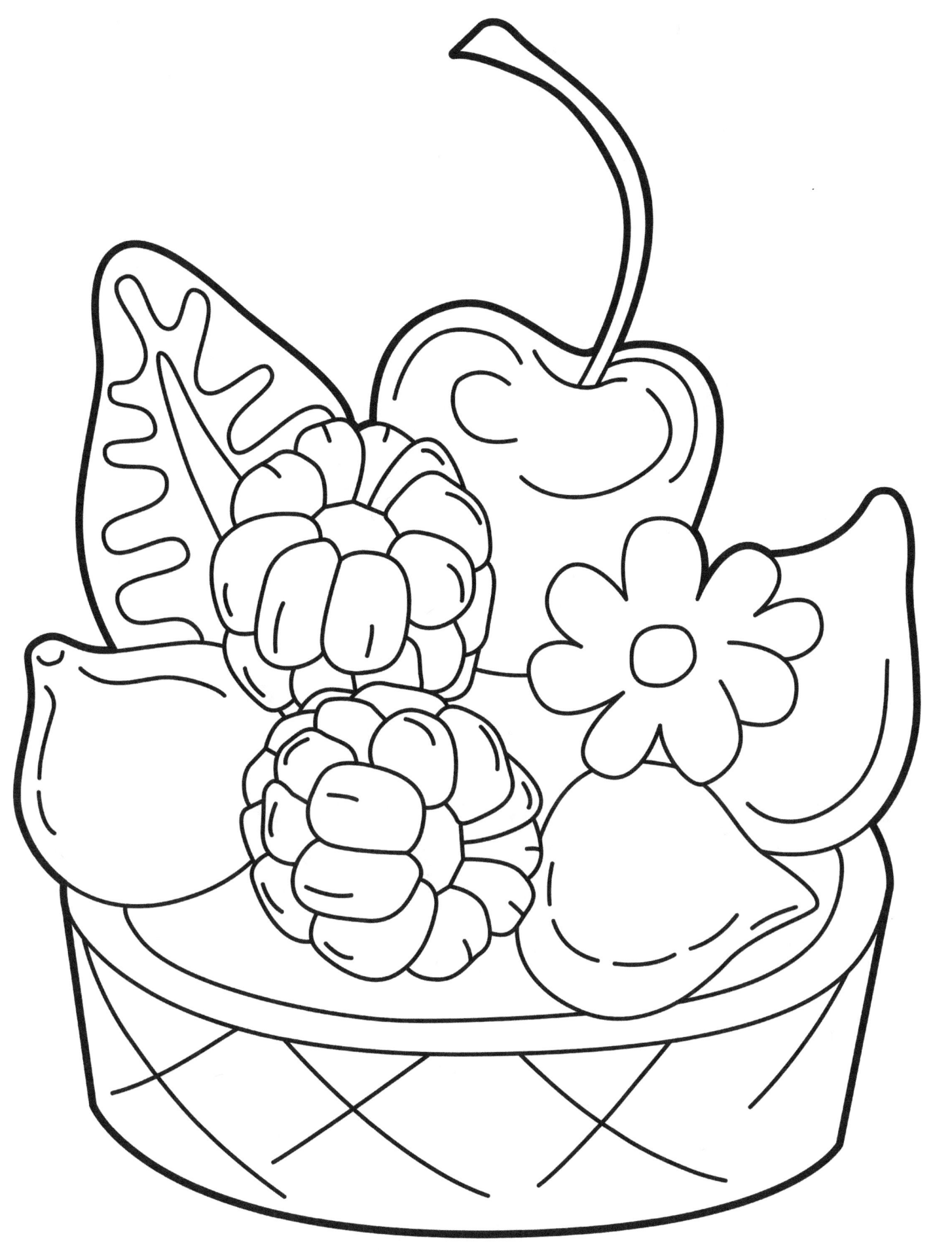

Adorable food
Coloring Book

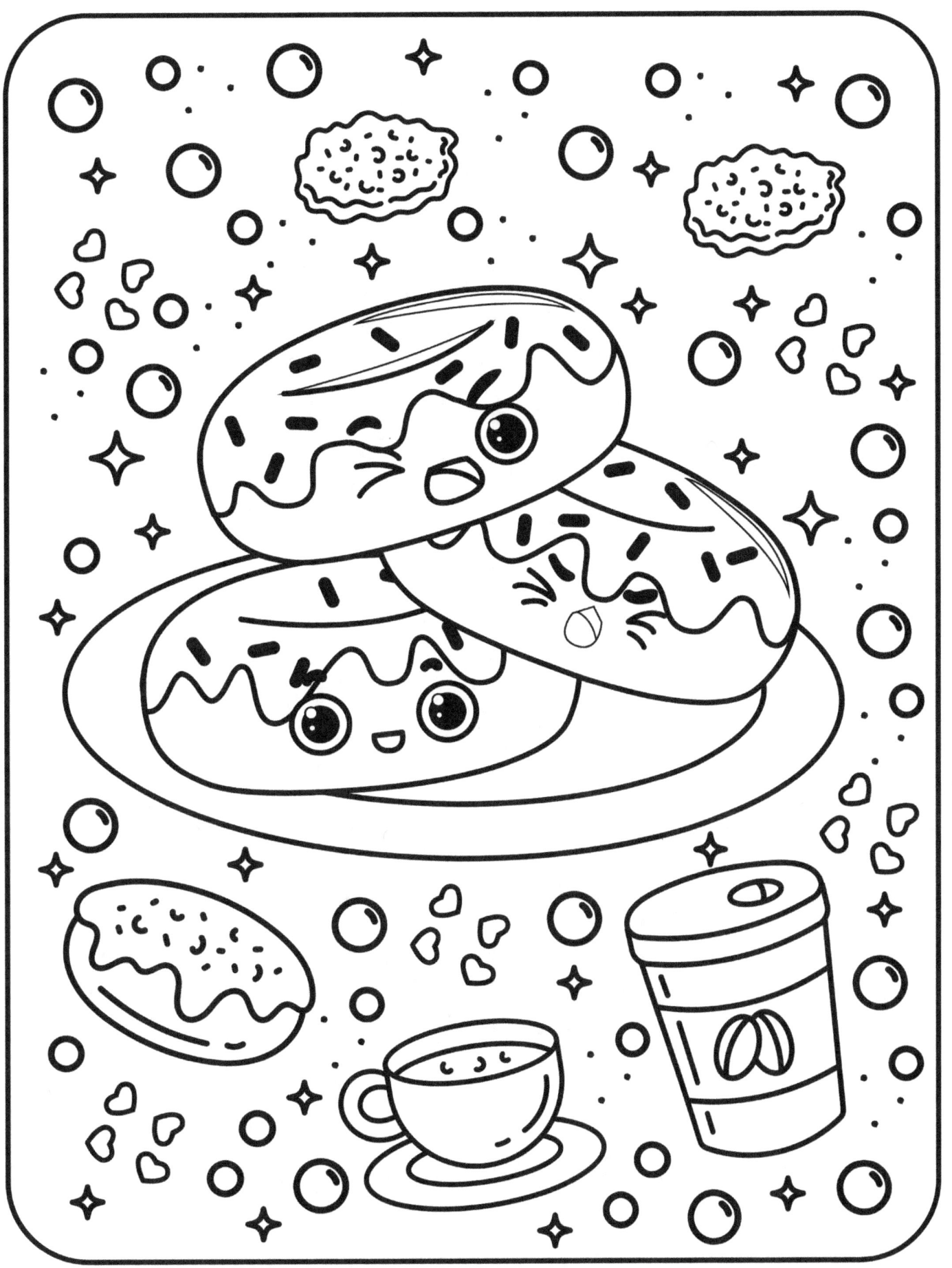

Adorable food
Coloring Book

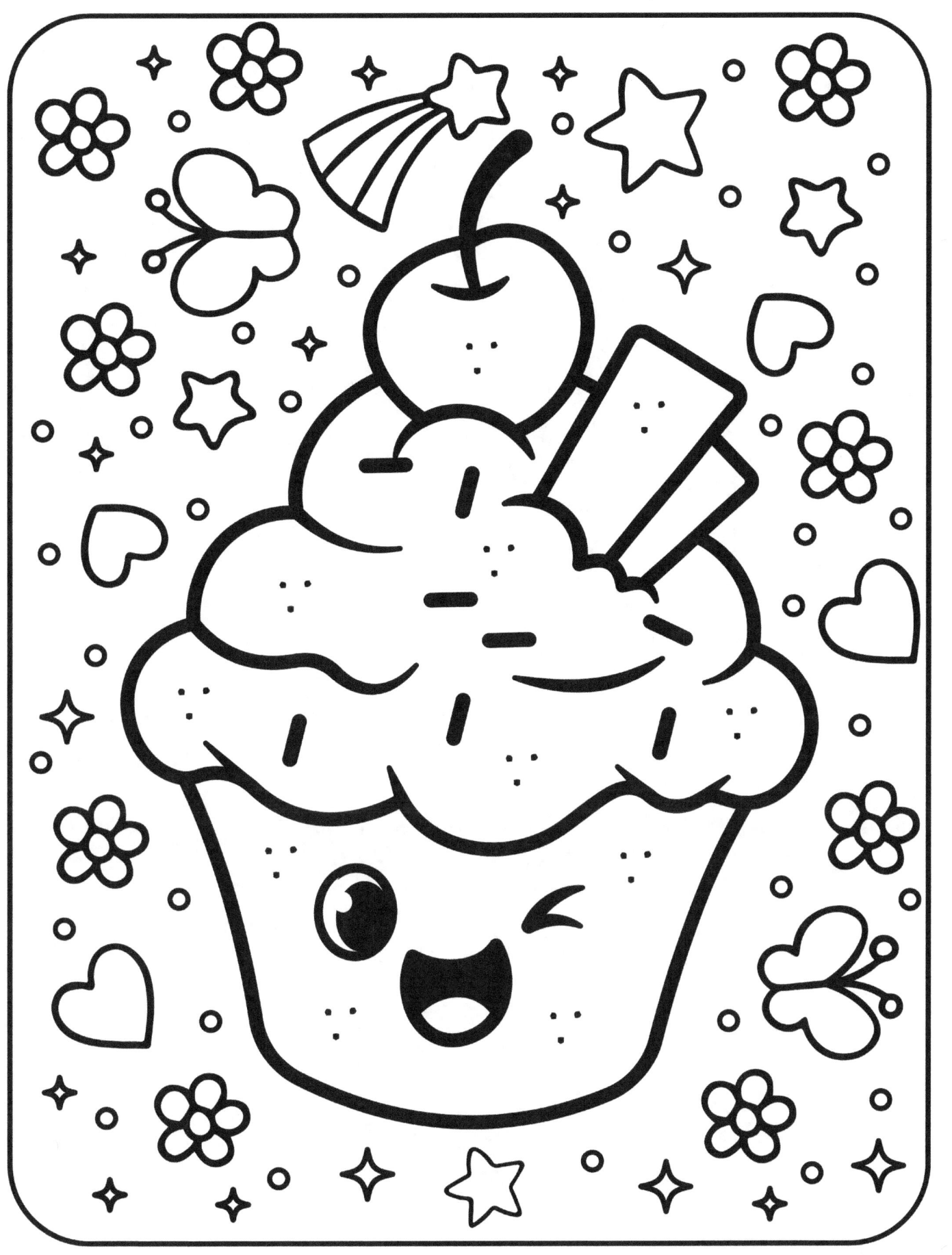

Adorable food
Coloring Book

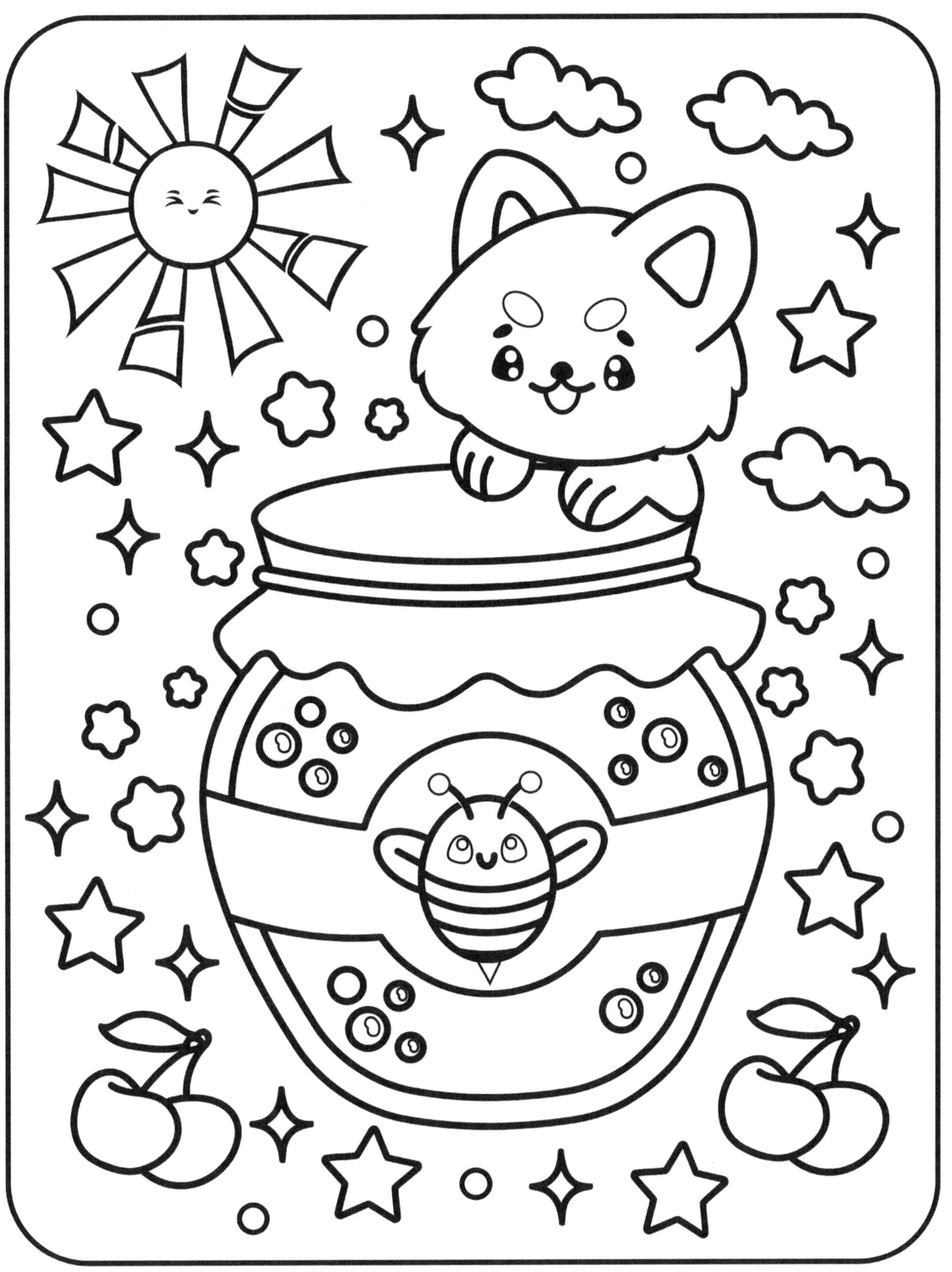

Adorable Food
Coloring Book

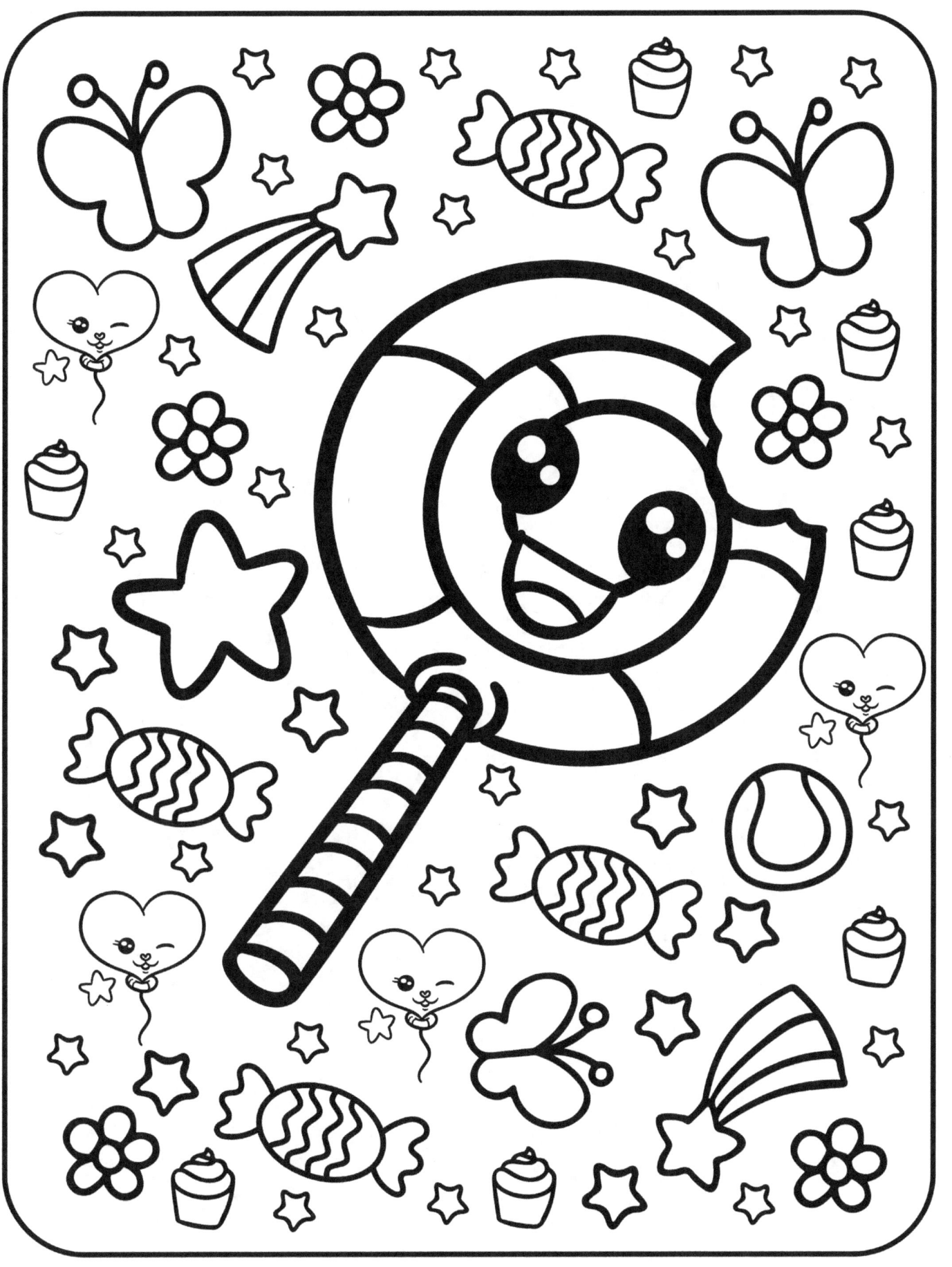

Adorable food
Coloring Book

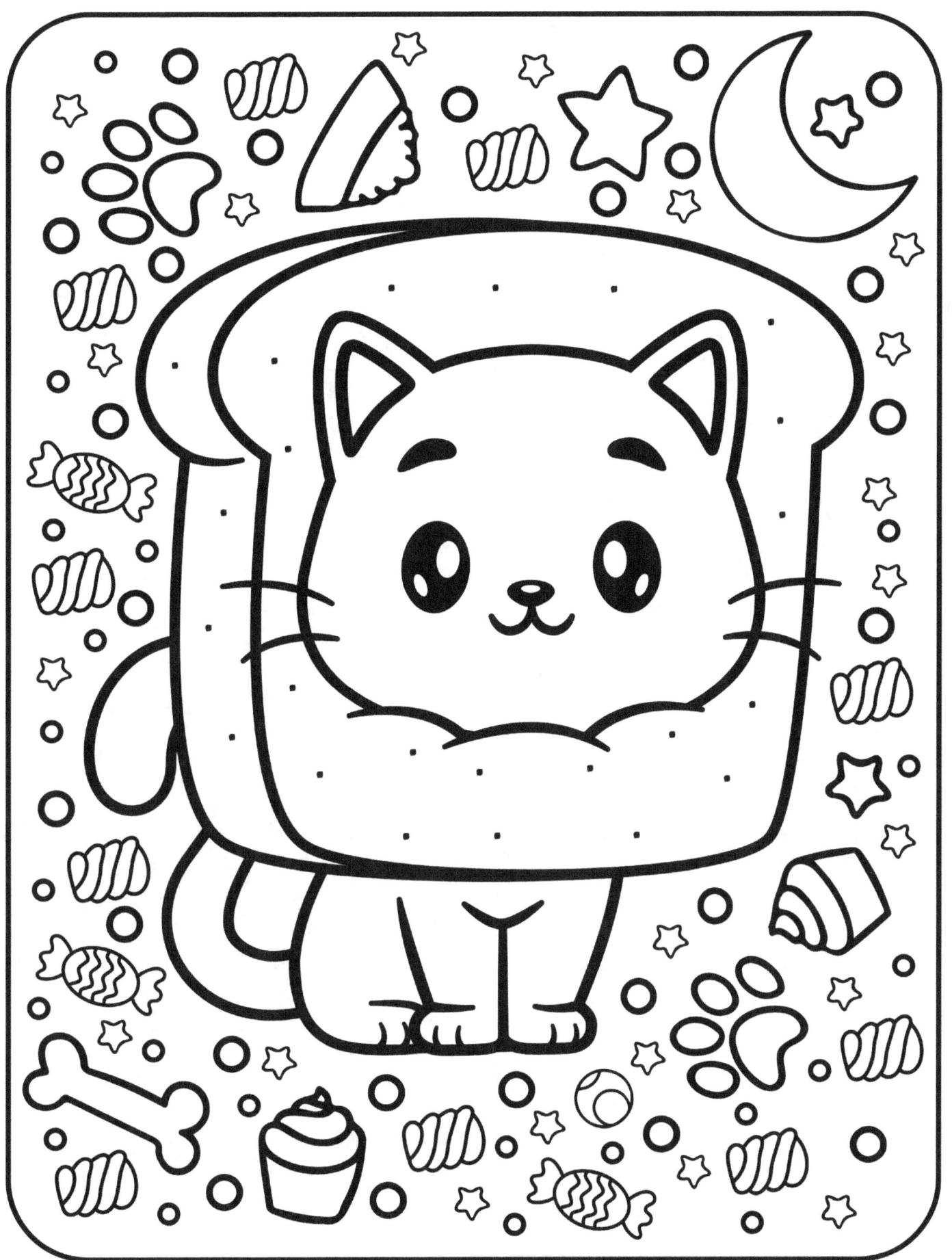

Adorable food
Coloring Book

Adorable food
Coloring Book

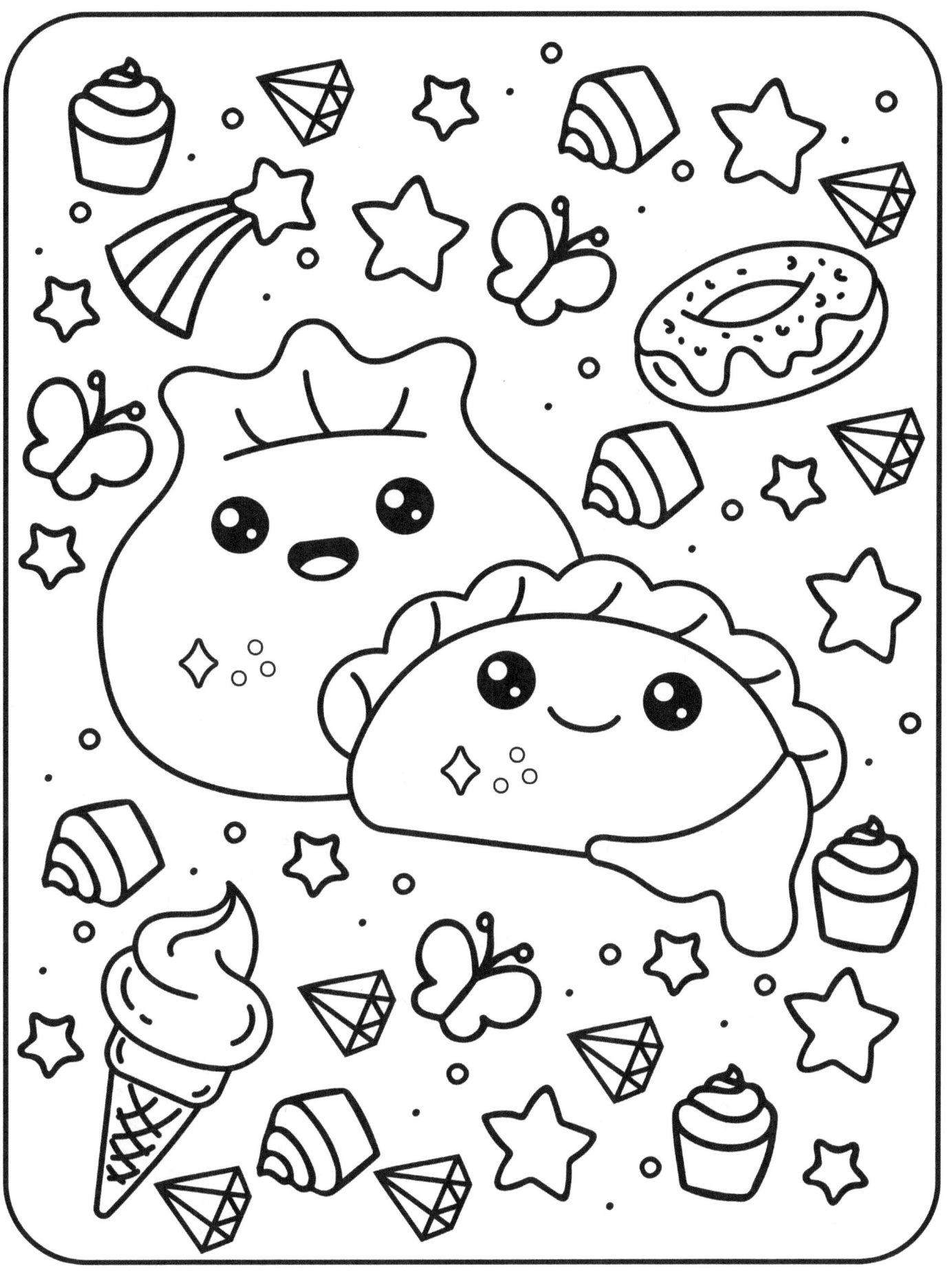

Adorable food
Coloring Book

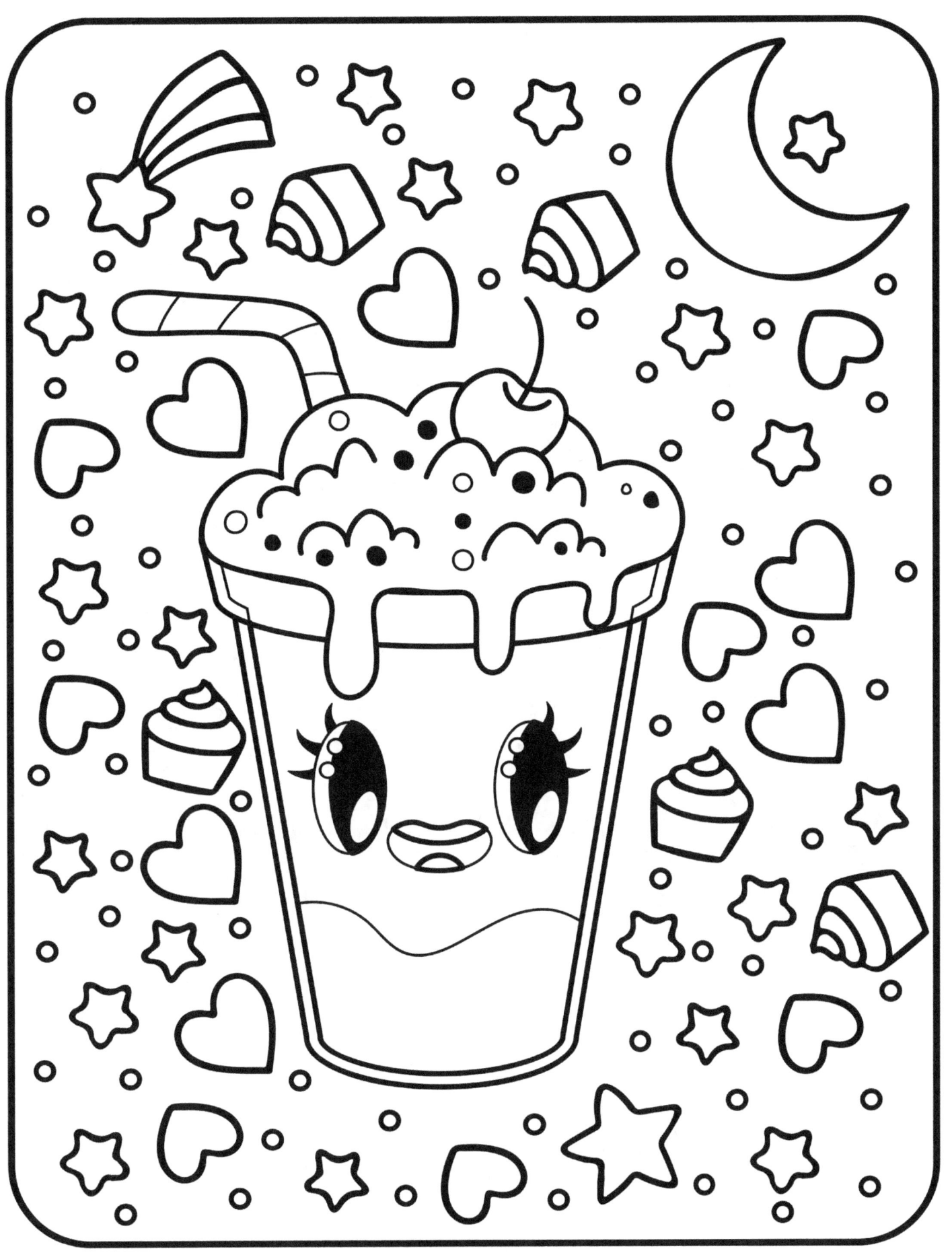

Adorable food
Coloring Book

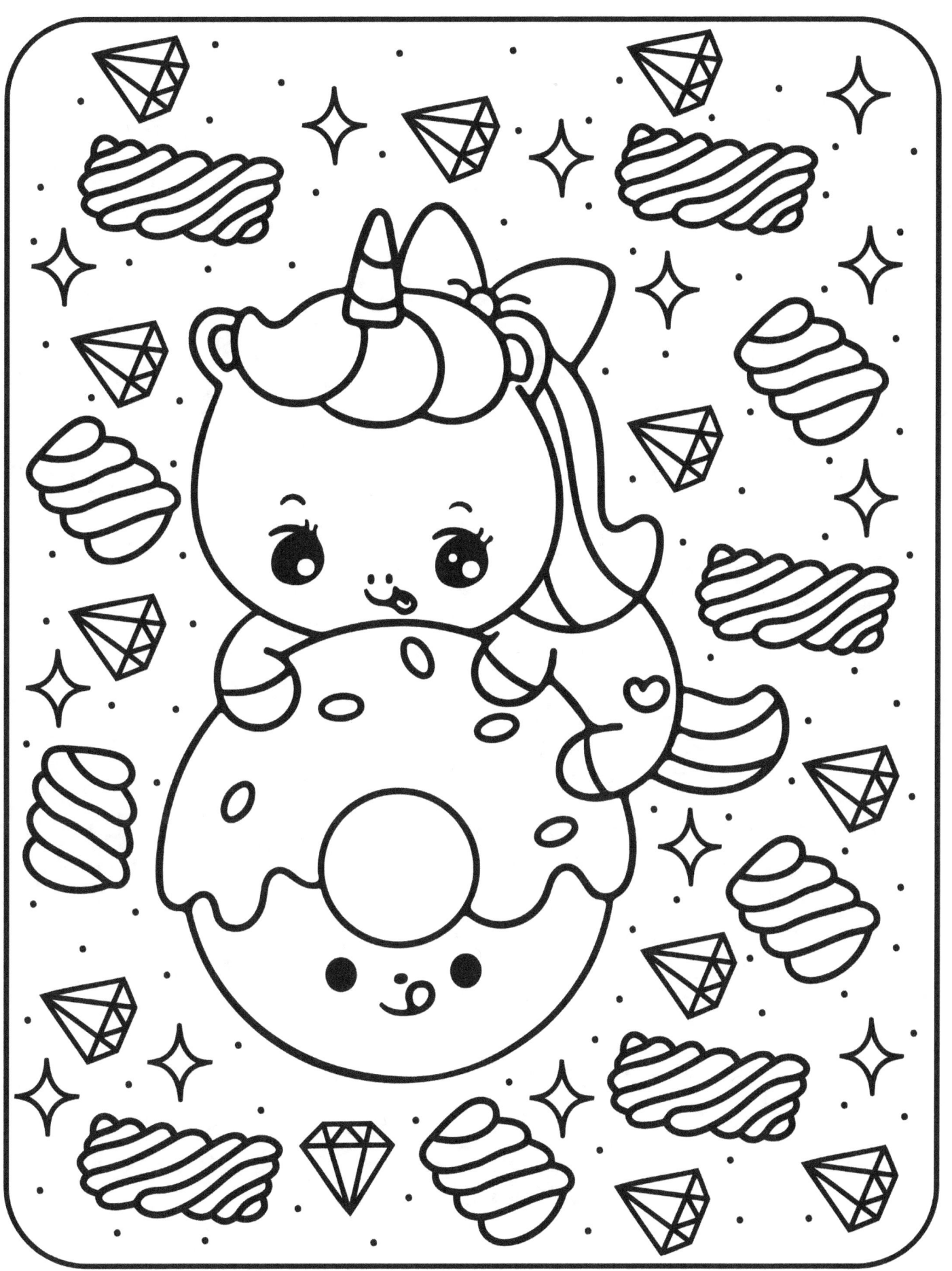

Adorable food
Coloring Book

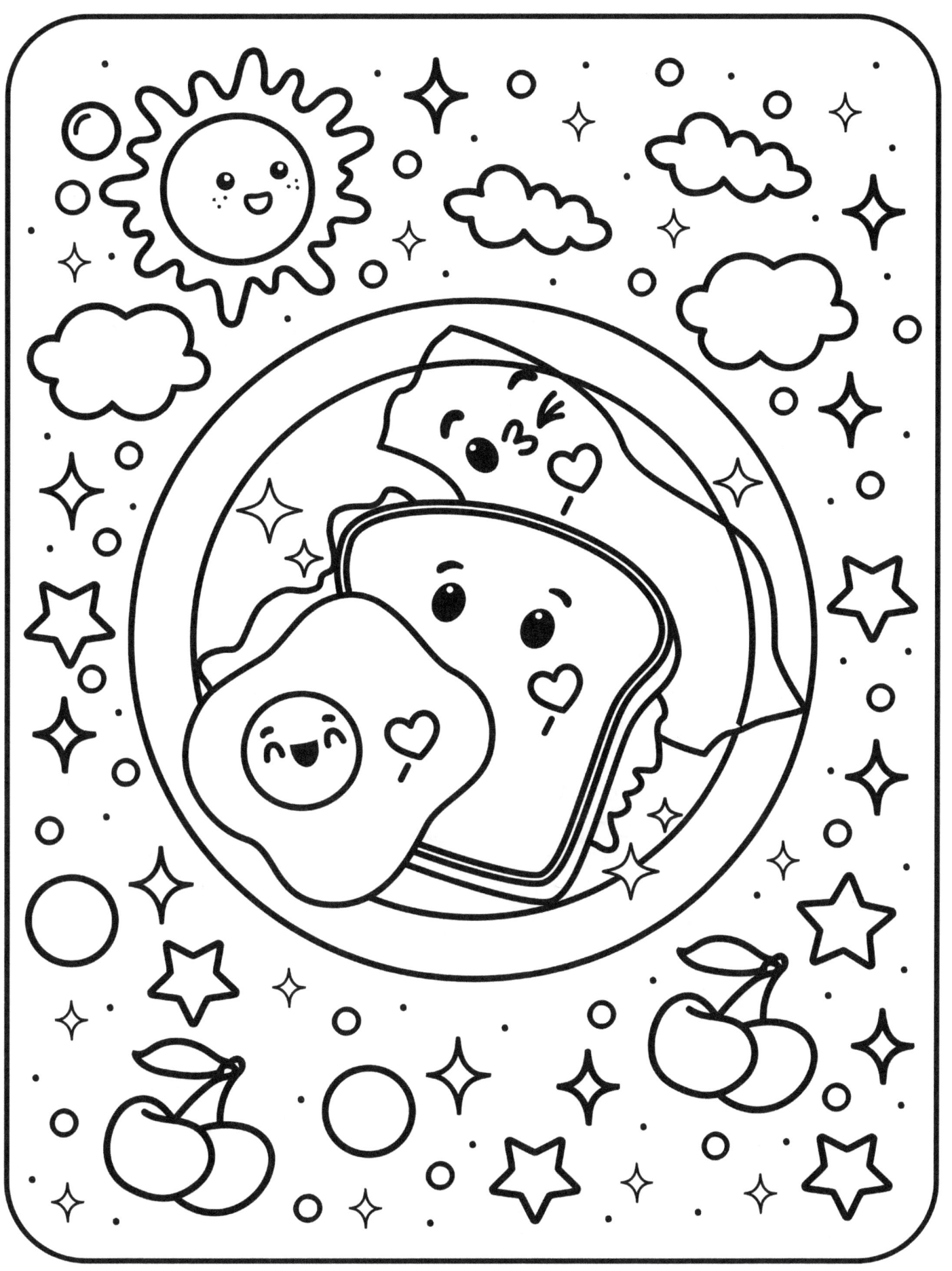

Adorable food
Coloring Book

Adorable food
Coloring Book

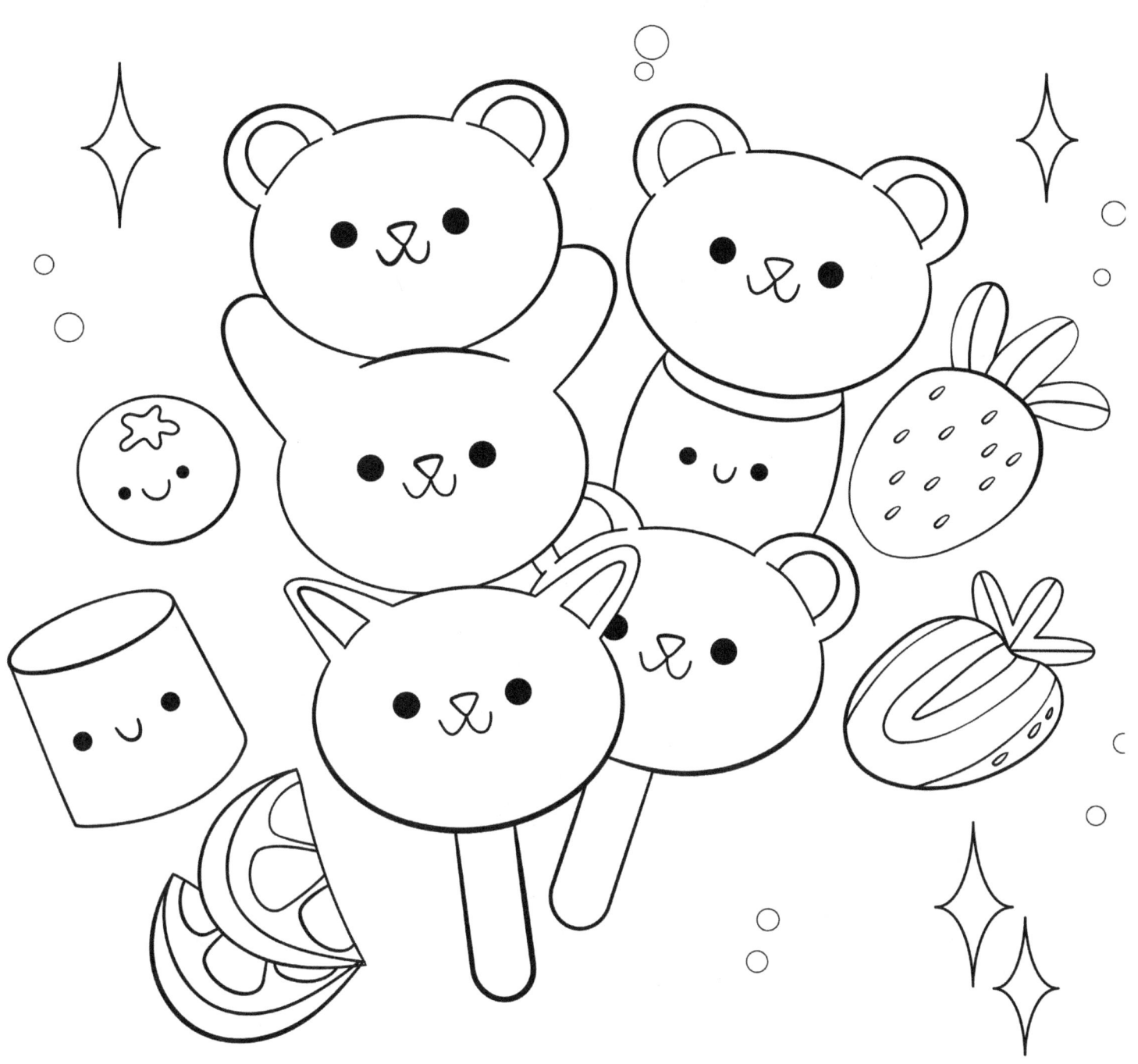

Adorable food
Coloring Book

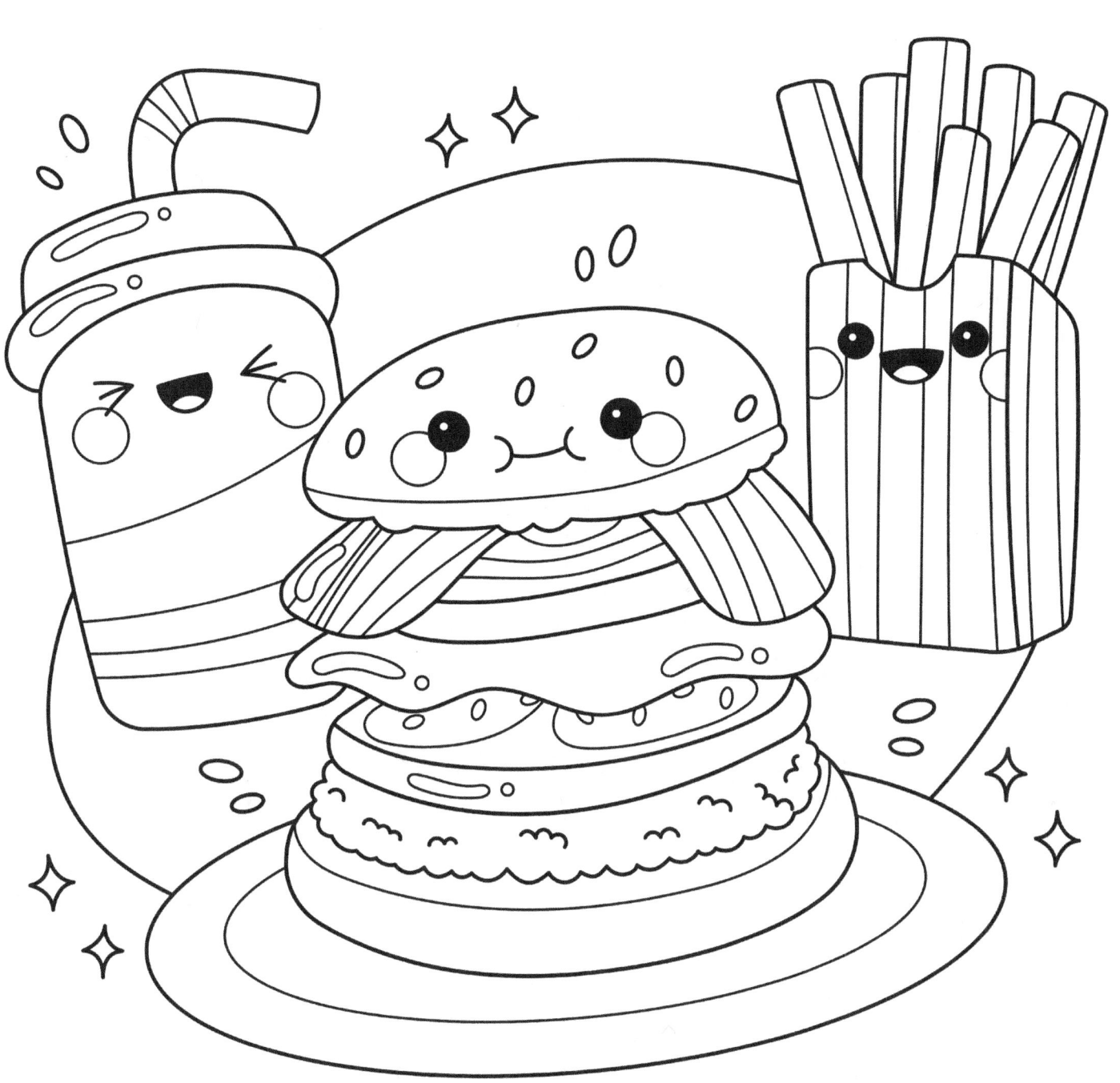

Adorable food
Coloring Book

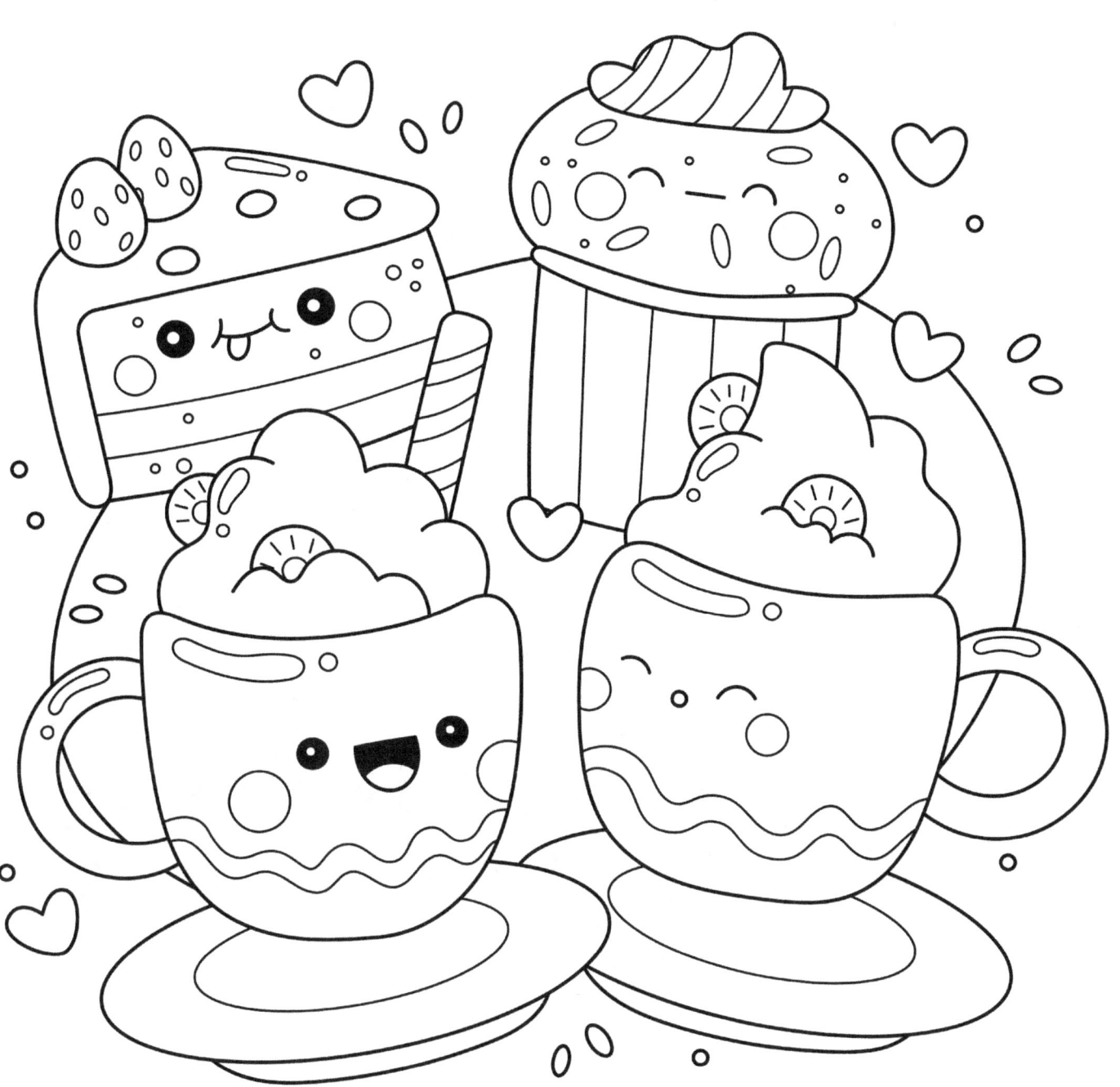

Adorable food
Coloring Book

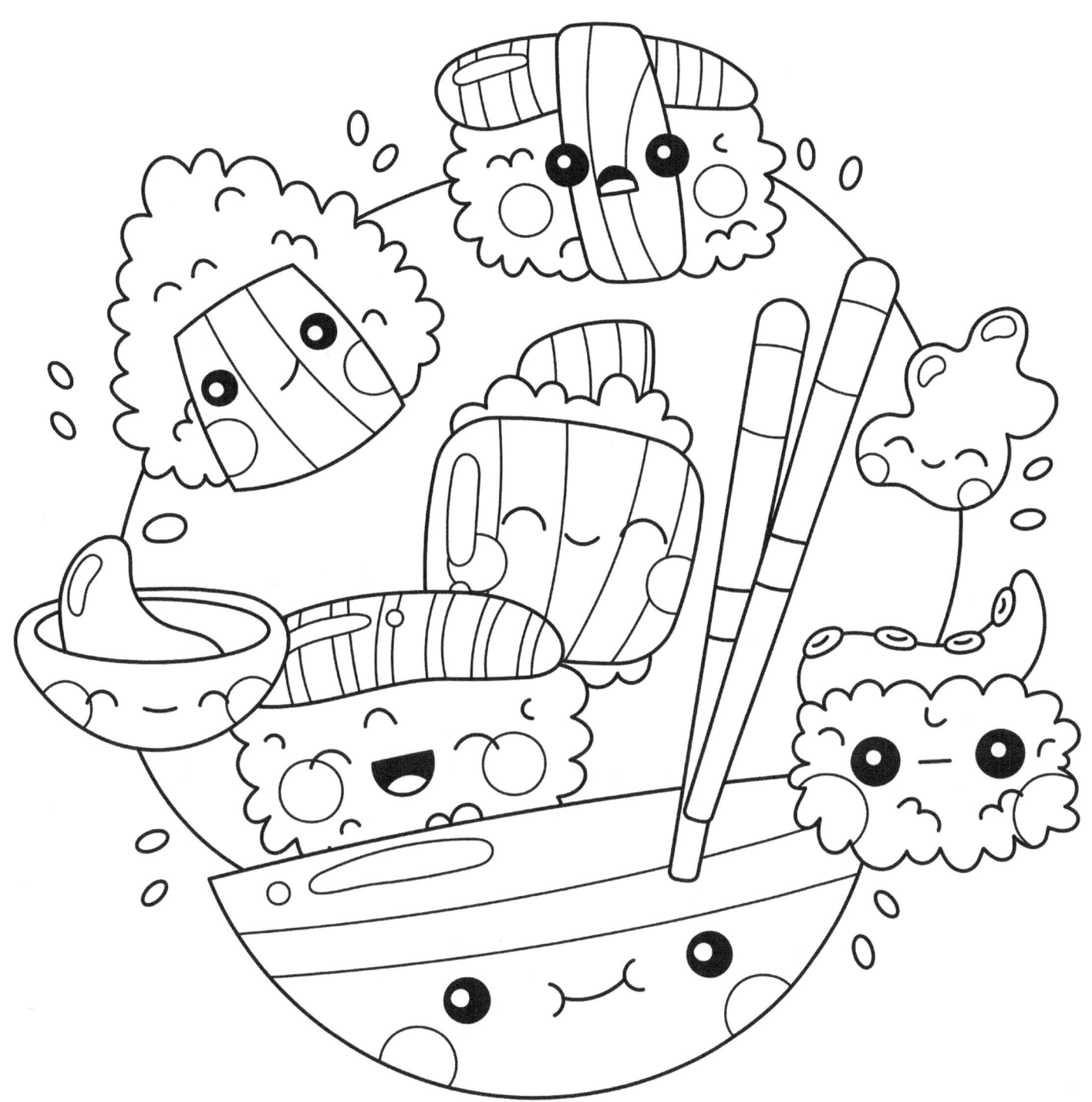

Adorable food
Coloring Book

Adorable food
Coloring Book

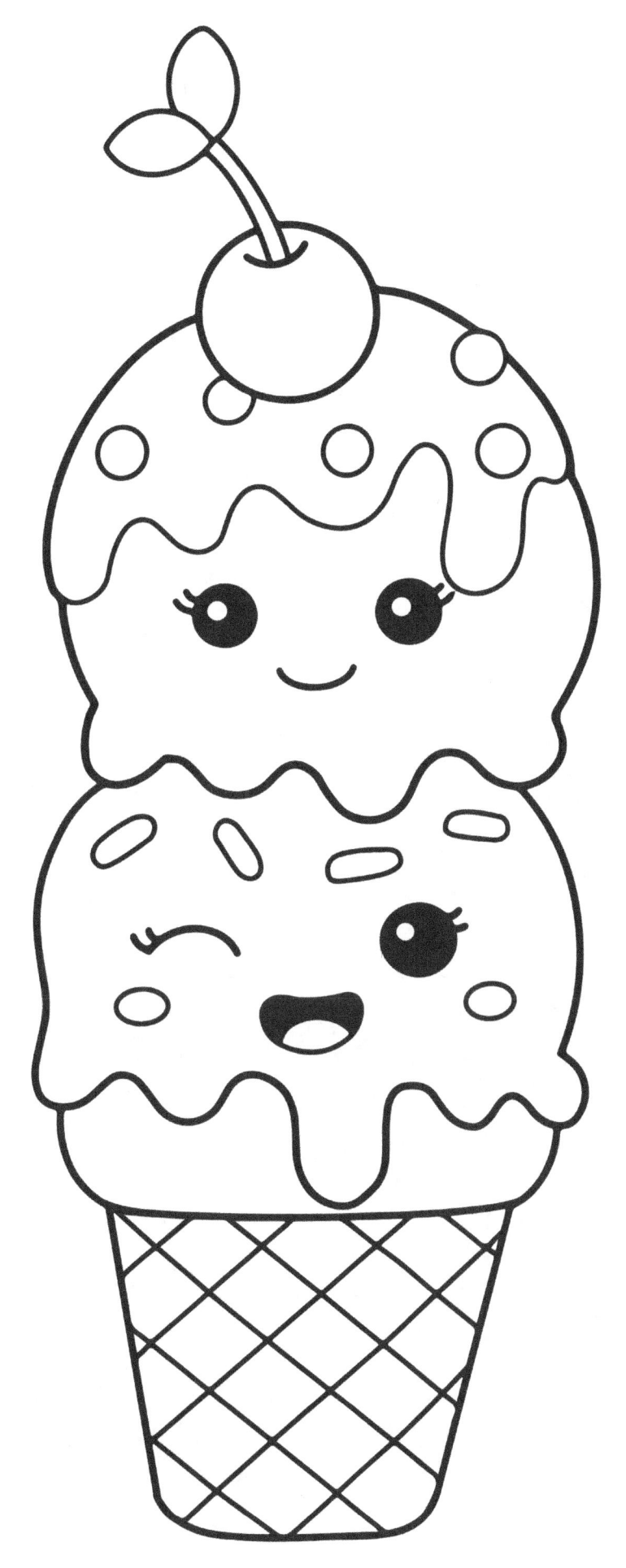

Adorable food
Coloring Book

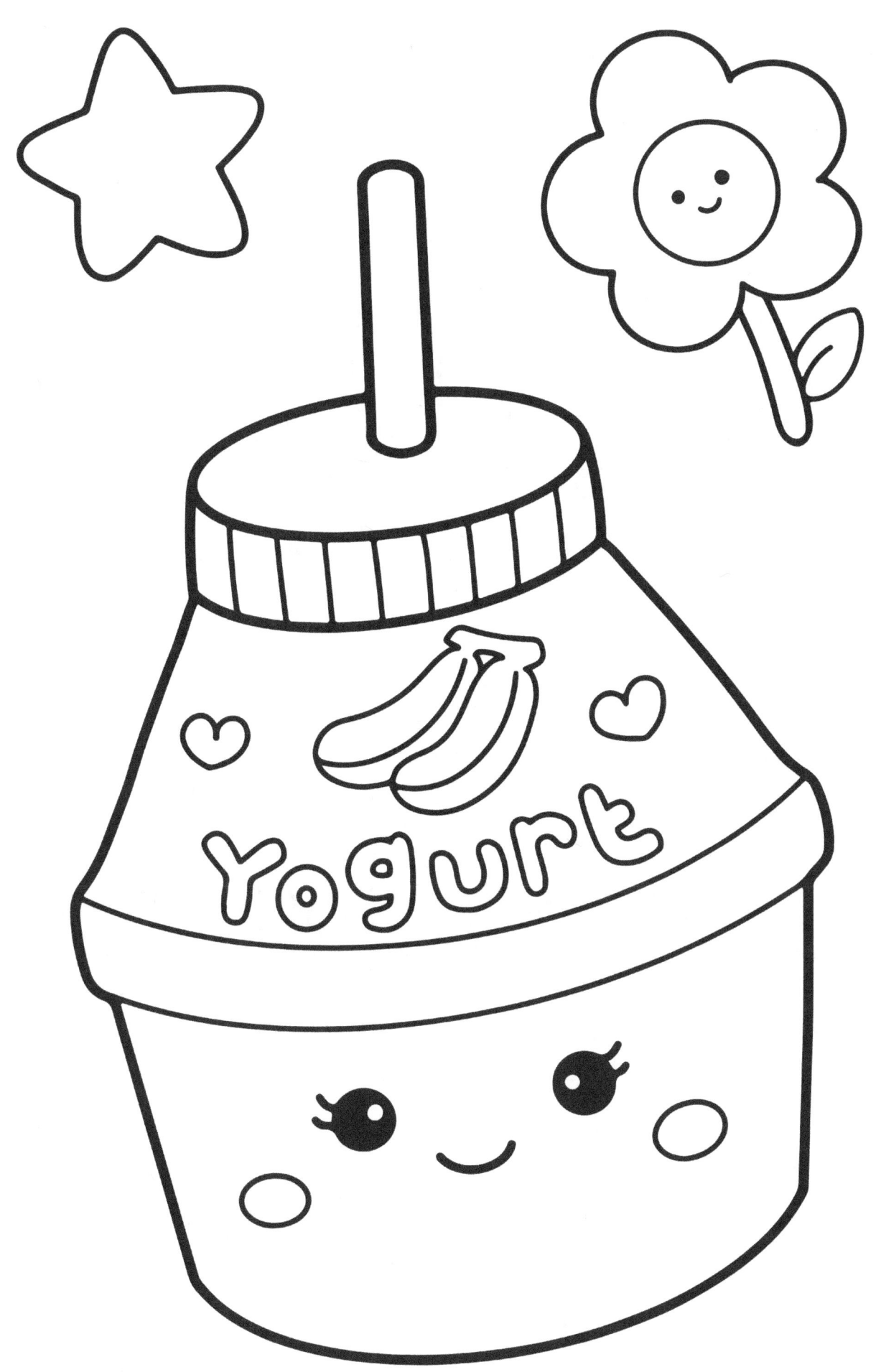

Adorable food
Coloring Book

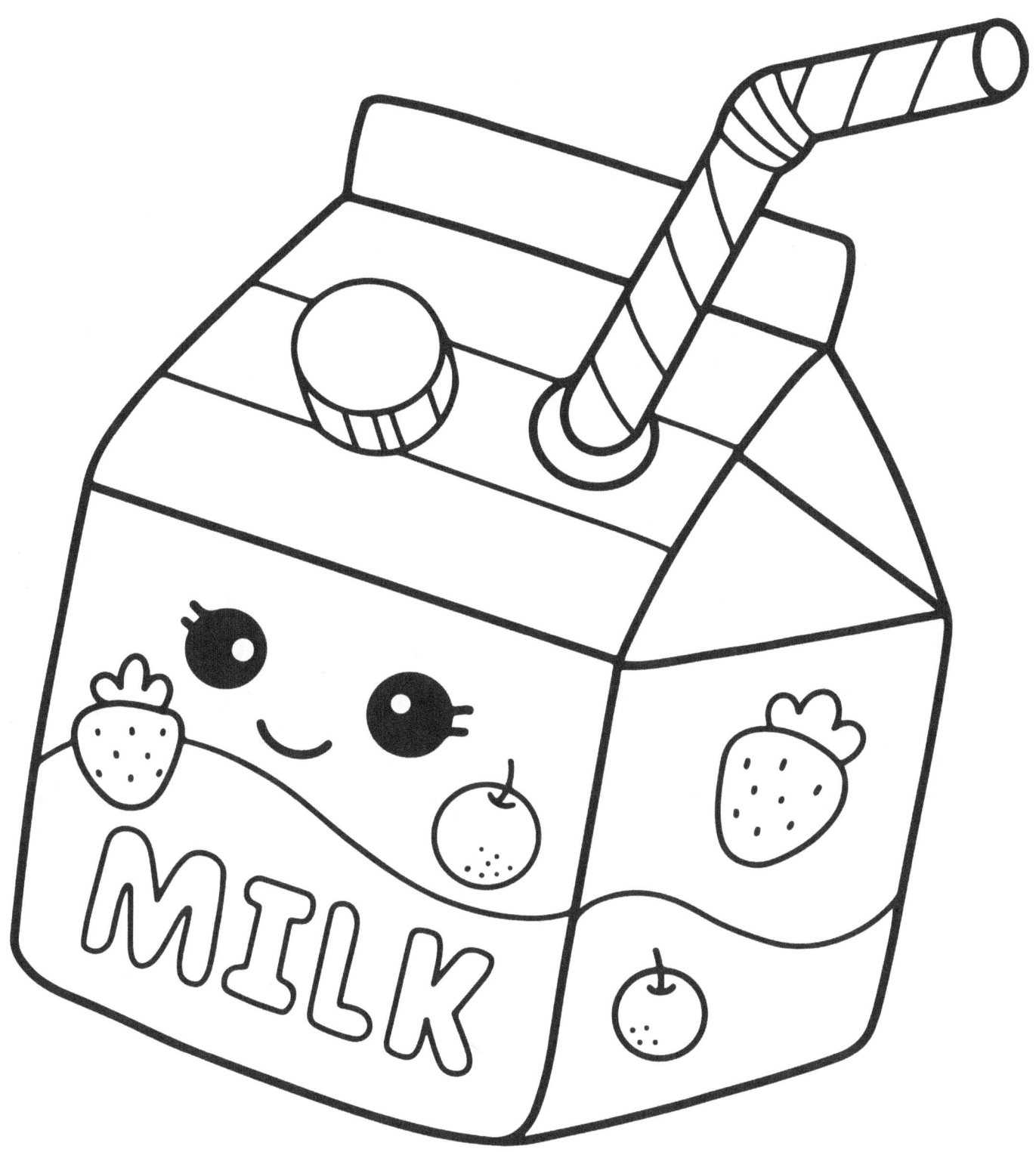

Adorable food
Coloring Book

Adorable food
Coloring Book

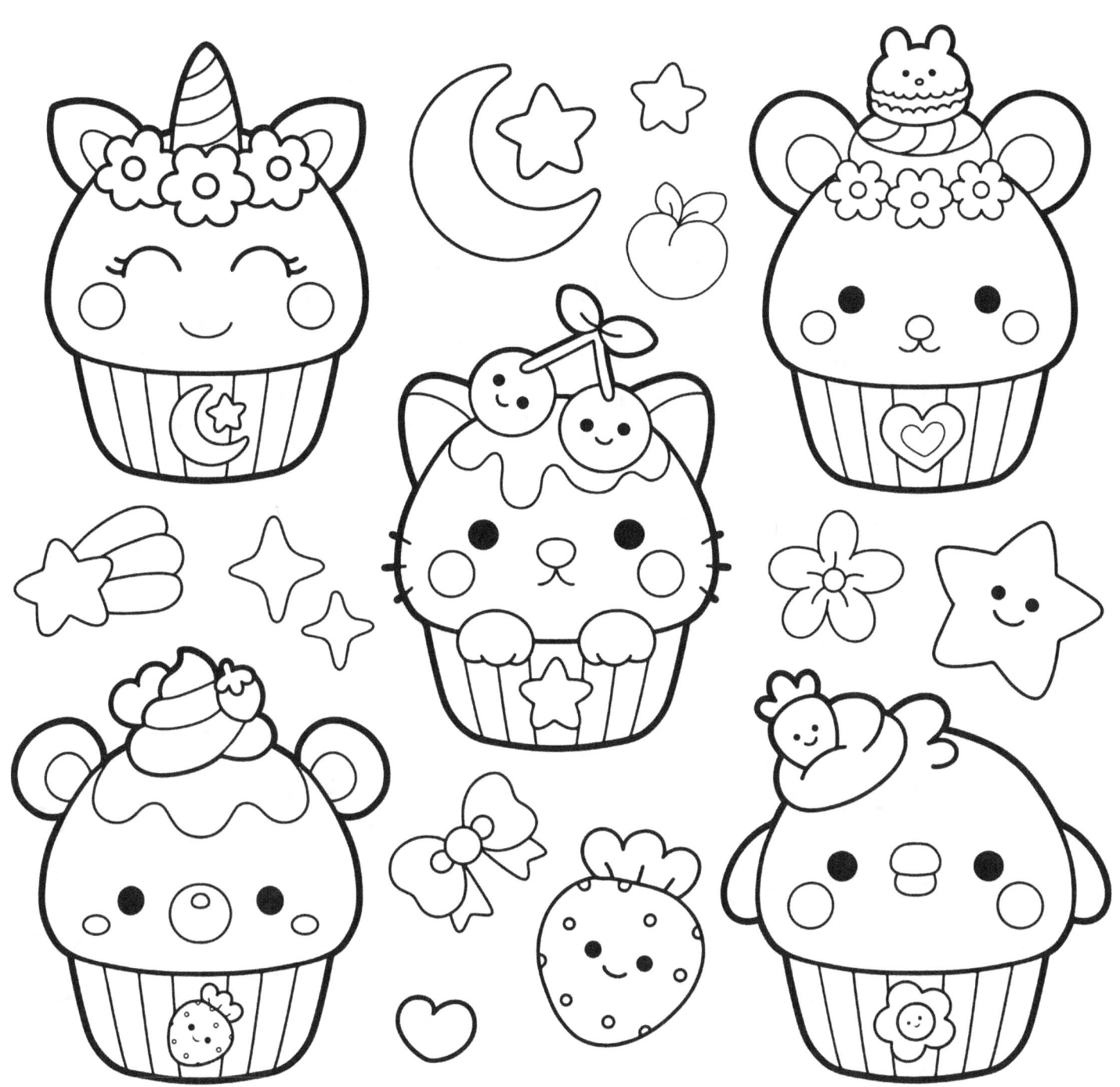